INTERFACT

THE BOOK AND DISK THAT WORK TOGETHER

SOLAR SYSTEM

TWO CAN ™

CHANHASSEN, MINNESOTA • LONDON

www.two-canpublishing.com

Published by Two-Can Publishing,
18705 Lake Drive East, Chanhassen, MN 55317

www.two-canpublishing.com

Created by
act-two
346 Old Street
London EC1V 9RB

ISBN 1-85434-904-X

4 6 8 10 9 7 5 3

A catalogue record for this book is available from the British Library

Photograph credits: Science Photo Library/Lynette Cook: front cover; NASA: pp.6–7, p.13, p.14,
p.15, p.17 (top right), p.19, p.21, p.23 (top right), p.23 (top left), p.34, p.35; NASA/Starland
Picture Library: pp.10–11, p.17 (top left); Julian Baum: pp.18–19, p.20, pp.22–24; US
Naval Observatory: p.25; Ian Graham: p.26. All illustrations by Chris Forsey and Peter Bull,
except those on pages 28–32, which are by Graham Humphries of Virgil Pomfret Artists.

Every effort has been made to acknowledge correctly and contact the source of each
picture and Two-Can Publishing apologises for any unintentional errors or
omissions which will be corrected in future editions of this book.

Printed in Hong Kong by Wing King Tong

INTERFACT

THE BOOK AND DISK THAT WORK TOGETHER

INTERFACT will have you hooked in minutes –
and that's a fact!

The disk is full of interactive activities, puzzles, quizzes and games that are fun to do and packed with interesting facts.

Use your knowledge of the solar system to rescue Alan the Astronaut.

Click to continue.

Open the book and discover more fascinating information, highlighted with lots of full-colour illustrations and photographs.

How does the Sun create so much energy? Read up and find out!

To get the most out of **INTERFACT**, use the book and disk together. Look out for the special signs, called Disk Links and Bookmarks. To find out more, turn to page 43.

23

BOOKMARK

DISK LINK
Label all the parts of a comet when you play
HERE COMES THE COMET!

Once you've clicked on to **INTERFACT**, you'll never look back.

LOAD UP!
Go to **page 40** to find out how to load
your disk and click into action.

3

What's on the disk

Welcome to the

INTERFACT

disk on the Solar System

To have a look at all the different things on the disk, simply click the arrow keys with your mouse.

As you do this, you'll see a description of each activity in the reading box.

Click on the picture at the top of the screen to select the activity you want to investigate.

HELP SCREEN

Learn how to use the disk in no time at all.

Get to grips with the controls and find out how to use:

- arrow keys
- reading boxes
- 'hot' words

You have arrived at Jupiter.

ROCKET MISSION

Are you ready for a journey into the depths of space?

Take command of your spacecraft and blast off on a voyage of cosmic discovery. The solar system is yours to explore! Visit any planet you choose and learn all about it.

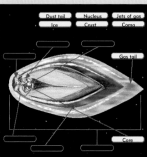

Dust tail Nucleus Jets of gas
Ice Crust Coma

Gas tail

Core

HERE COMES THE COMET

Examine a comet close-up.

Take a close look at a cross section of a comet and try to label its different parts. Find out more about each one and hunt for facts hidden on screen.

LOST IN SPACE

Have you got what it takes to be a galactic whizz kid?

Test your brains in a quiz that's out of this world. Alan the Astronaut is lost in space. Use your knowledge of the solar system to rescue him.

SHUTTLE SECRETS

Snoop around an interactive illustration of the Space Shuttle!

Welcome aboard the Space Shuttle – take a look around! Use your mouse to explore the world's first re-useable spacecraft and find out everything you've ever wanted to know.

OUT OF THIS WORLD

Find out the answers to all your cosmic questions!

Do you know how big the solar system is? To find out, just ask the Robotic Answering Device. Get the lowdown on meteors, asteroids, galaxies and the Sun!

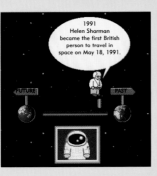

TIME LINE

Travel through time and explore the history of astronomy and space travel!

Watch Astro get older or younger as you slide him along the Time Line. See how our knowledge of the universe has changed through the ages.

METEOR MADNESS

Use your brain power to save the Earth from destruction!

Answer questions then use your sharp shooting skills to blast the meteorites before they hit Earth. Are you smart enough to save the planet?

What's in the book

*All words in the text which appear in **bold** can be found in the glossary*

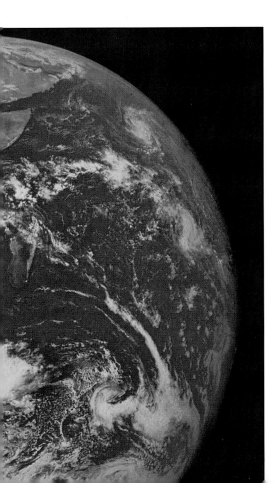

Our solar system

Our solar system is made up of the Sun and everything that orbits it. The planets, the **moons** that circle the planets and a variety of other objects, including **comets**, move the way they do because of the Sun's **gravity**.

There are nine planets. Our planet, Earth, is the third in line from the Sun. The planets are all quite different. Their differences are largely the result of their different distances from the Sun.

The four planets that are closest to the Sun are called the inner planets. They are small rocky worlds. The outer planets, with the exception of Pluto, are larger and gassy. All but two planets, Mercury and Venus, have moons in orbit around them.

▼ The Sun contains more than 99 per cent of all the mass, or material, in our solar system.

1. Mercury 6. Sun
2. Venus   7. Saturn
3. Earth   8. Uranus
4. Mars   9. Neptune
5. Jupiter 10. Pluto

SOLAR SYSTEM FACTS

- The orbits of the planets lie roughly in a flat plane, except for Pluto's, which is tilted at a greater angle than the others.

- All of the planets orbit the Sun in the same direction.

- Our solar system is about 12,000 million km across.

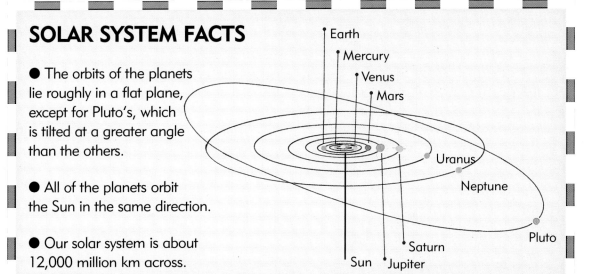

Earth
Mercury
Venus
Mars
Uranus
Neptune
Pluto
Sun   Jupiter   Saturn

DISK LINK
Our solar system is part of a galaxy. To find out more about galaxies, ask RAD in **OUT OF THIS WORLD.**

The Sun

The Sun is a star. Compared to many other stars in the night sky, it is quite ordinary. Other stars are bigger or smaller, hotter or colder than the Sun. To us, the Sun seems to be the biggest star of all, but this is only because it is the nearest star to Earth.

The Sun is a huge ball of gases, mainly hydrogen and helium. At its centre, the temperature and pressure are so great that hydrogen **atoms** are forced together to form helium atoms by a process called nuclear fusion. When this happens, a huge amount of **energy** is released into the solar system in the form of heat and light. The Earth receives only a tiny fraction of the Sun's total energy output but this is still enough to warm the Earth and to provide the light that all green plants need to survive.

● The Sun is 1.4 million km across and the temperature at its core is 15 million °C.

DISK LINK
The Sun is divided into six layers. To learn more about the Sun's layers, play ROCKET MISSION.

The Sun's core

◀ Eruptions on the Sun's surface can throw out gas in an arch called a prominence. Sun flares send out high-speed particles that interfere with radio signals on Earth.

▶ The corona, the Sun's outermost layer, extends millions of kilometres into space. The glowing corona is easily visible when the Moon passes between Earth and the Sun.

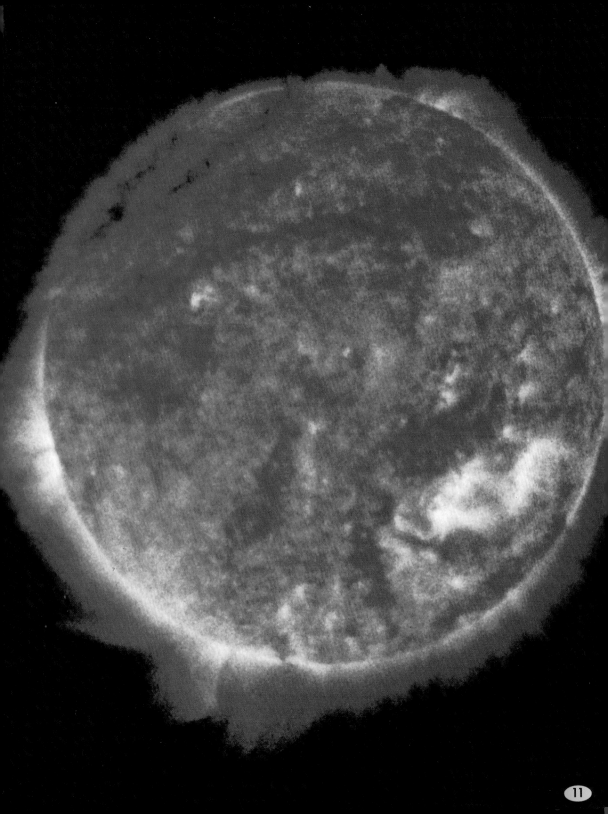

The Earth and Moon

Our own planet, Earth, is the only planet in the solar system where life has been discovered. It is also the only planet that has flowing water on its surface. Almost three-quarters of Earth's surface is covered by water.

The pull of Earth's **gravity** traps a layer of air called the **atmosphere** around the planet. Earth's rocky surface, or crust, is not as solid and stationary as it seems. It consists of a number of separate plates that move. Where they meet, these plates rub against each other. This is what causes **earthquakes** and **volcanoes**. Earth's surface is also changed by the action of wind, rain and the tides.

▲ The Moon's gravity is only one-sixth of Earth's and it is unable to hold an atmosphere.

EARTH FACTS

● Earth's core is made of iron and nickel and has a solid centre and a liquid outer core. Around this is a layer of rock called the mantle, with a thin layer of rock on top, Earth's crust.

● The layer of gases that lies between our planet and outer space is Earth's atmosphere. Earth formed from material orbiting the Sun about 4.5 thousand million years ago.

MOON FACTS

● The Moon is the only other place in the solar system apart from Earth where man has set foot. Between 1969 and 1972, a total of 12 astronauts landed on the Moon.

DISK LINK
What were Neil Armstrong's words as he set foot on the Moon? Find out in TIME LINE.

The tides – the twice-daily rise and fall in sea levels – are mostly caused by Earth's satellite, the Moon. As the Moon orbits Earth, its force of gravity pulls on the water directly under it and so raises the water level.

▲ Earth's blue oceans, brown land masses and white cloud make it one of the most colourful planets in our solar system. This photograph was taken from space by a weather satellite orbiting Earth at a height of 36,000km.

Mercury and Venus

Mercury is the closest of the nine planets to the Sun. The Sun is two-and-a-half times bigger in Mercury's sky than it is in Earth's sky. The side of Mercury that faces the Sun is heated to more than 400°C, which is hot enough to melt lead. However, as the planet turns away from the Sun, the night-time temperature plunges to –170°C.

MERCURY FACTS

● Mercury's day, the time it takes to rotate, is 59 Earth-days long. Its year, the time it takes to orbit the Sun, is 88 Earth-days long. So on Mercury, a year is only one-and-a-half days long!

When the US space probe Mariner 10 flew past Mercury in 1974–1975, it sent back pictures of a rocky planet, a third of the size of Earth and covered with craters that looked like our Moon's.

Venus is nearly the same size as Earth, but it is a very different world. Its **atmosphere** contains mainly carbon dioxide and its clouds contain droplets of sulphuric acid. The pressure at its surface is nearly 100 times the pressure at Earth's surface.

DISK LINK
Long ago, there may have been oceans on Venus. Remember this when you're LOST IN SPACE!

◀ This picture of Mercury was taken by Mariner 10 in March 1974. It shows Mercury's heavily cratered surface.

▶ This photograph of Venus shows the planet's thick covering of cloud. The US Magellan probe used **radar** to look through the cloud and see the surface.

VENUS FACTS

● The former Soviet Union landed space probes on Venus and taken pictures of its rocky surface. Its sky is orange-yellow.

● Venus is the brightest object in the night sky apart from the Moon.

Mars

The planet Mars has fascinated people for thousands of years. Some ancient civilisations worshipped it as a god, and it is in fact named after the Roman god of war.

In 1877, an Italian astronomer named Giovanni Schiaparelli drew a map of Mars. It caused great excitement because the planet was shown criss-crossed with what Schiaparelli described as channels.

In the early 1900s, the US astronomer Percival Lowell also saw the channels, but he described them as "man-made canals". For the next 70 years or so, scientists could not agree whether or not intelligent creatures lived on Mars. In the 1970s, space probes visited Mars to investigate. As a result, it was finally proved that there are no canals or intelligent life there at all.

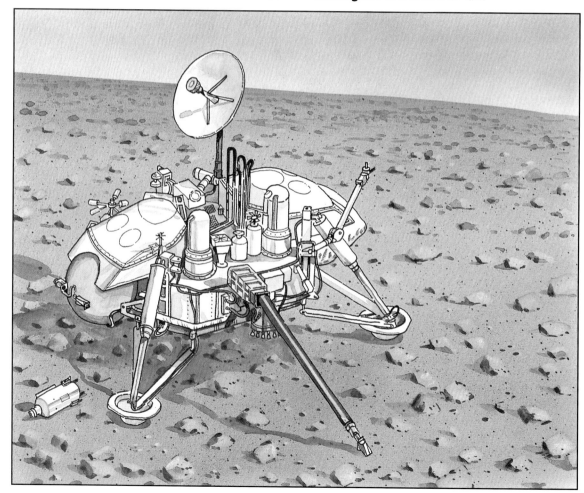

▶ This photograph of Mars taken from Earth shows one of its polar icecaps, but little else. More detailed studies of Mars were made possible by space probes.

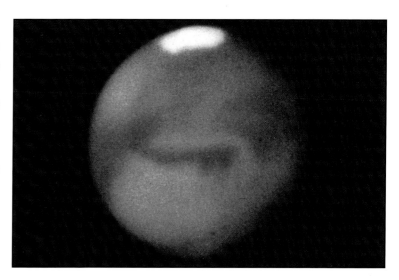

▼ Mars is also known as the Red Planet. It has a huge **volcano** called Olympus Mons. This is 25km high and 600km across.

◀ A US Viking Lander sits on Mars. Two Viking spacecraft landed on Mars in 1976. They took photographs and tested the soil for signs of life.

MARS FACTS

● Mars' **diameter** is half of Earth's. Its force of **gravity** is weaker. If you weighed 50kg on Earth you would weigh only 19kg on Mars.

● A Martian day is only a few minutes longer than an Earth-day, but the Martian year is 687 Earth-days.

● Mars looks like a red star in the sky. It is brightest every 780 days when it is on the other side of the Sun from Earth. Mars has two **moons**, called Phobos and Deimos.

DISK LINK
How hot is the temperature on Mars? Blast off in ROCKET MISSION and find out!

Jupiter

Jupiter is the giant of our solar system. Earth would fit inside this vast planet more than 1,300 times! Jupiter is unlike the rocky inner planets. It is a huge ball of liquid wrapped in gas clouds. It is mostly made of hydrogen and helium, just like a star. In fact, Jupiter seems to be a star that failed to 'turn on'. It was unable to attract enough material to create the high temperature and pressure at its core that is necessary for nuclear fusion to begin.

Jupiter's most obvious feature is its Great Red Spot. This is caused by a storm in the planet's **atmosphere**. The first person to observe the Great Red Spot was probably Robert Hooke – and that was nearly 350 years ago!

▼ Until US probes flew past the outer planets, only Saturn, Neptune and Uranus were known to be encircled by rings. Then the Voyager spacecraft also discovered rings around Jupiter (below).

DISK LINK
Who discovered moons around Jupiter in 1610? Find out in TIME LINE.

PAST

JUPITER FACTS

● Jupiter is bigger and heavier than all the other planets added together.

● Jupiter has **16 moons**. One of them is larger than the planet Mercury.

Earth

● Jupiter's rotation is rapid. This planet takes less than ten hours to rotate.

◀▼ Three huge, oval clouds formed around the Great Red Spot in 1940. You can see one of them in the picture below. On the left, an artist's impression shows a probe plunging into the planet's clouds.

Saturn

Saturn, with its flattened disc of rings, is the most spectacular planet in our solar system. The rings change in appearance depending on whether they are tilted towards Earth or have their edges facing Earth. They seem to disappear when seen from the side. Saturn is the second biggest planet in the solar system. Like Jupiter, it is mostly liquid hydrogen. Saturn has 18 **moons**. The largest moon, Titan, has a thick **atmosphere** of nitrogen gas.

▶ This picture shows Saturn and its largest moons. The Voyager space probe discovered that the planet's broad rings were actually hundreds of narrow ringlets.

SATURN FACTS

● Saturn is twice as far from the Sun as Jupiter so it is much colder. It receives only one-hundredth as much heat from the Sun as Earth does.

● Saturn is over 120,000km across. That is almost ten times the **diameter** of Earth.

Earth

▲ Some of the ringlets around the planet Saturn are held in place by the **gravity** of nearby moons. Astronomers have nicknamed these moons 'shepherd satellites'.

DISK LINK
If you want to save the Earth in METEOR MADNESS, remember what you read!

Uranus, Neptune, Pluto

Uranus, Neptune and Pluto are the most distant planets from the Sun. Uranus is tilted on its axis as it **orbits** the Sun, making it appear to lie on its side. Uranus' poles are a great deal hotter than its **equator**, which must produce very odd seasons. Neptune was thought to be similar to Uranus until the Voyager 2 space probe found it to be a much stormier planet.

Neptune's largest **moon**, Triton, has an **atmosphere** and a **magnetic field** – two features of a planet. It may have been a small planet that was caught by Neptune's **gravity**. Pluto's orbit is tilted at a greater angle to the orbits of the other planets. It also crosses inside Neptune's orbit.

▼ Voyager 2 passed within 82,000km of the clouds surrounding Uranus.

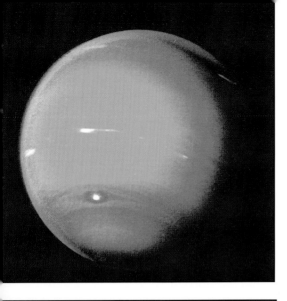

▲ Above left, by photographing Neptune through filters, Voyager measured the amount of methane gas in its atmosphere. Above right, an artist's impression of Pluto, its moon Charon and the distant Sun.

COLD FACTS

● Uranus and Neptune consist of a ball of hydrogen and helium gases with a rocky core surrounded by ice. They are almost the same size, roughly 49,000km in **diameter**.

● Pluto's diameter is 2,300km and it is the smallest planet in the solar system.

DISK LINK
Visit all the planets on this page when you take part in ROCKET MISSION!

Comets, asteroids and meteors

A broad band of asteroids lies roughly between the orbits of Mars and Jupiter. The largest asteroids are up to 1,000km across and are known as minor planets. They seem to be the ingredients of a planet that failed to come together.

▼ During the 1990s, the Galileo space probe orbits Jupiter to study the planet. It is shown here passing an asteroid.

DID YOU KNOW?

● Not all asteroids are found in the asteroid belt. The Apollo asteroids orbit near the inner planets. Several have passed within a few million kilometres of Earth. The Trojan asteroids are trapped in Jupiter's orbit where the Sun's and Jupiter's **gravity** balance.

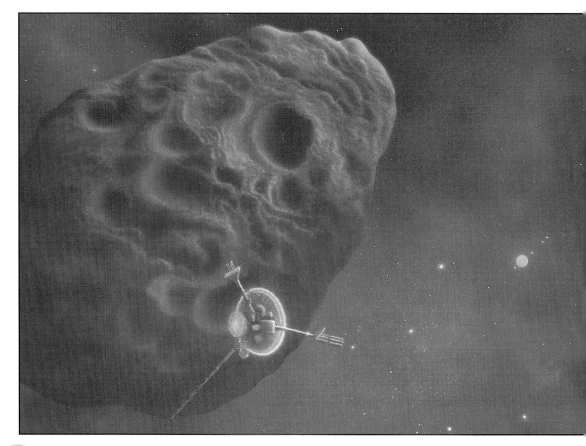

Comets and meteors can often be seen from Earth. Comets are balls of dusty ice that orbit the Sun. The head of a comet is called the nucleus. Gas evaporating from the nucleus forms the comet's tail, known as the coma. The force of solar wind blows the tail away from the Sun. A meteor is a streak of light that is seen in the night sky for a moment and then disappears. Meteors are produced when small particles of rock enter Earth's **atmosphere** and burn up.

▼ Comet Ikeya-Seki was visible with the unaided eye several times in 1975. The coma and tail can be seen very clearly.

DISK LINK
What's the difference between a meteor and a meteorite? RAD has the answer in OUT OF THIS WORLD.

Space probe

Unmanned space probes, such as the Pioneer and Voyager spacecrafts, have explored vast expanses of our solar system. They have sent back photographs and information by radio from hundreds of millions of kilometres away.

We know a great deal more about the Sun, the planets, their **moons** and even the origin of our solar system thanks to deep space probes. The two Voyager space probes sent back more than 30,000 photographs from Jupiter alone.

They then went on to visit most of the outer planets.

DISK LINK
What is a Space Shuttle and how does it work? Find out with the help of SHUTTLE SECRETS!

▼ A space probe nears Saturn. Its dish aerial receives commands and sends back information to Earth.

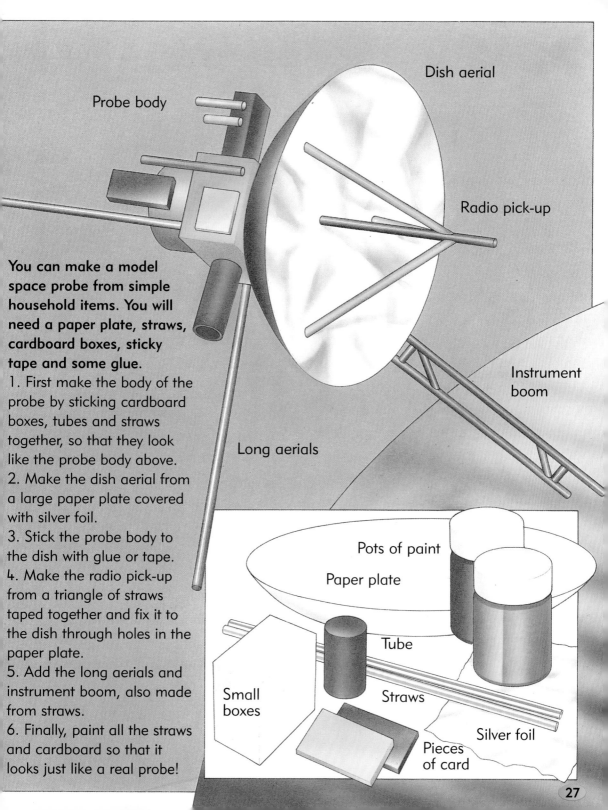

Probe body

Dish aerial

Radio pick-up

Instrument boom

Long aerials

You can make a model space probe from simple household items. You will need a paper plate, straws, cardboard boxes, sticky tape and some glue.

1. First make the body of the probe by sticking cardboard boxes, tubes and straws together, so that they look like the probe body above.

2. Make the dish aerial from a large paper plate covered with silver foil.

3. Stick the probe body to the dish with glue or tape.

4. Make the radio pick-up from a triangle of straws taped together and fix it to the dish through holes in the paper plate.

5. Add the long aerials and instrument boom, also made from straws.

6. Finally, paint all the straws and cardboard so that it looks just like a real probe!

Pots of paint

Paper plate

Tube

Small boxes

Straws

Silver foil

Pieces of card

A journey through our solar system

Ever since modern and more powerful rockets began to be developed in the 1950s, people have imagined journeys to distant planets and beyond. This true-to-life story about a journey into space is set in the year 2050 when it is expected that space travel will be quite commonplace.

"Crossing Saturn's orbit," the ship's electronic voice purrs from the loudspeaker in the corner of the cabin. Most of the passengers go to the windows, hoping to catch a glimpse of the ringed planet. The passengers are all science officers who are returning to Earth after a five-year tour of duty at the Deep Space Observatory. This is a space station permanently in orbit around the planet Neptune.

They are travelling in the ferrycraft, Solar Explorer 2. The spacecraft's engines work by heating liquid hydrogen in a nuclear reactor. The engines provide the initial acceleration to move the craft out of Neptune's orbit and to make course corrections, but for most of the journey, the craft 'coasts' unpowered. It uses the pull of gravity of the various planets to help to bring it back to Earth.

Hydrogen-powered turbines generate the craft's electricity. When the craft is closer to the Sun, solar panels can be used, but in the outer reaches of the solar system there is not enough sunlight for them to work efficiently.

The cylindrical middle section of the 150m-long spacecraft spins just fast enough to produce a force similar to Earth's gravity against its outer wall. To the people on board this section, 'up' is towards the centre of the spacecraft.

However, the flight deck, where the pilot, commander and engineering officer work, does not spin. As these members of the crew are consequently weightless, they have to be strapped into their seats while they work. This prevents any unnecessary accidents while the crew float around the deck.

"Over here," shouts someone. The passengers all rush to the windows. In the far distance, Saturn lies like a glowing, golden ball on a black, velvet sheet. Its flattened disc of rings is tipped over towards the spacecraft showing off the rings at their best. The spacecraft's forward video camera slowly rotates to point at the planet. The screen shows that there are actually hundreds of bright rings packed closely together.

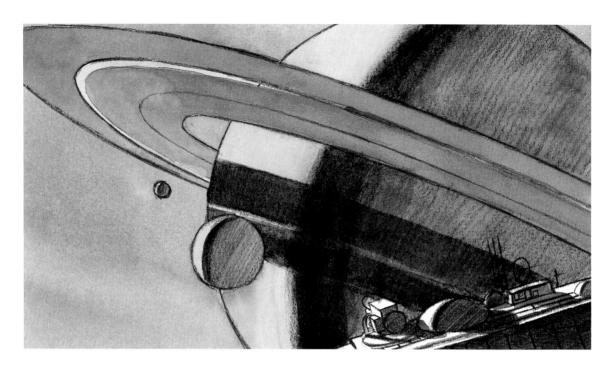

The flight attendant explains that they will not be so lucky with the next planet – Jupiter. By the time they reach Jupiter's orbit, the planet will be hundreds of millions of kilometres away on the other side of the Sun.

"It's going to be a long trip then," says one passenger.

The attendant nods. "Yes, flight time is estimated at 1,735 days – I calculate that to be four years and nine months." Jupiter is so massive that the extra acceleration from its gravitational field can make all the difference between a short and a long voyage.

Saturn disappears from the viewing screen and one of several safety and training films, shown to every group of passengers, begins. The passengers return to their seats and the presenter

explains the next stage of the flight.

"We will soon begin reducing speed to prepare for the asteroid belt." This is a region of space between the orbits of Mars and Jupiter, where millions of rocks orbit the Sun. It is a very dangerous area for any spacecraft. "In three hours, we will make a course correction that will pitch us up over the densest region of the belt," the presenter continues. "We will maintain our reduced speed until the positions and trajectories of all large objects in our vicinity are mapped. We will then be able to enter the asteroid field at the safest moment."

During an average journey through the asteroid belt, perhaps more than two dozen large chunks of rock come within sight of the spacecraft. These and many smaller objects are tracked by using

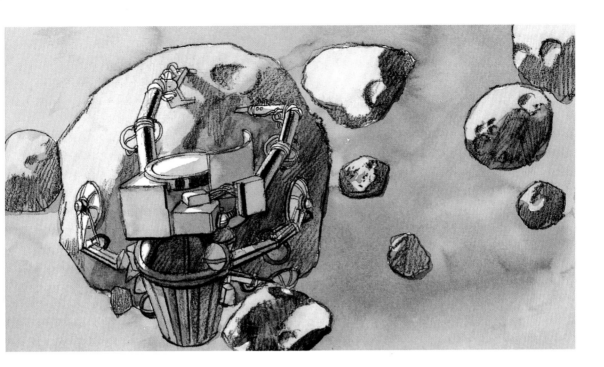

radar to ensure that none of them endanger the spacecraft.

The viewing screen begins to show a film of a spacecraft on a previous flight as it journeys through the asteroid belt. Large boulders glide across the screen. Some are as big as small planets. A small, grey spacecraft is highlighted against the yellow background of one of the larger asteroids.

"That's a miner," says one of the passengers. Asteroids rich in valuable minerals are mined by a fleet of mining craft. These operate from mother-ships that lie in safer space outside the asteroid belt. Once safely through the asteroid belt, Solar Explorer 2 sets course for Mars.

On such a long journey, passengers often become very bored. There is nothing to see through the observation windows apart from the occasional close approach to a planet. For most of the journey, there is nothing but darkness and stars outside.

Radio messages take so long to travel from Earth to the craft that two-way conversations are impossible. Most passengers record messages to be transmitted to Earth and then read, take exercise or watch video films while they wait for replies.

To make the journey pass more quickly, passengers can apply for a sleep pattern regulation programme. By wearing a cap fitted with electrodes, the passenger's brain waves can be modified to make him or her sleep longer – up to several days at a time – with no ill effects.

Soon after crossing the orbit of Mars, sleep pattern regulation is brought to an end. This is in order to give passengers plenty of time to adjust to normal day and night cycles before they arrive back on Earth. At its closest approach to Mars, Earth is only 56 million km away. The journey is nearing its end.

In common with all interplanetary spacecraft, the Solar Explorer will not land on Earth. It was not designed to withstand the high temperatures, forces and friction normally experienced by a spacecraft entering a planet's atmosphere. Instead, it will dock with a space station which is permanently in orbit around Earth. For the last stage of the journey home, the passengers will then transfer to a shuttle craft, which is more resistant to heat and pressure.

Excitement quickly grows among the passengers as Earth comes into view and two-way radio conversations become possible. The other planets of the solar system that have been passed by the Solar Explorer spacecraft are either violently stormy, hostile worlds or dead chunks of cratered rock. Compared to them, the bright sphere of the temperate Earth, covered by curling white swirls of cloud and deep blue oceans looks very welcoming.

True or false?

Which of these facts are true and which are false? If you have read this book carefully, you will know the answers!

1. Our solar system consists of the Sun, the planets, their **moons** and all objects trapped by the Sun's **gravity**.

2. The inner planets, the four planets that are closest to the Sun, are all small, rocky worlds.

3. Jupiter contains more material than all of the other planets put together.

4. Arches of gas, thrown out of the Sun's surface are called prominences.

5. The Sun is a huge ball of gases. It contains a wide variety of different gases, but it consists mostly of carbon dioxide and oxygen.

6. We always see the same side of the Moon because it does not spin round.

7. Saturn's famous rings are solid discs of frozen hydrogen and water-ice mixed with particles of dust blown by winds.

8. Tides are caused by the solar wind blowing water against the shore.

9. Most asteroids lie between the orbits of Mars and Jupiter.

ANSWERS: 1.T 2.T 3.T 4.T 5.F 6.T 7.F 8.F 9.T

Glossary

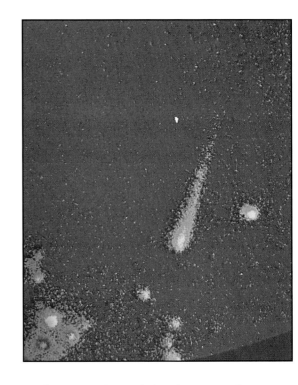

Atmosphere is a layer of gas that surrounds some stars, planets and moons. The Earth's atmosphere is roughly four-fifths nitrogen and one-fifth oxygen, with tiny amounts of a few other gases. Other planets, such as Neptune, have different types of atmosphere.

Atoms are the basic units that make up everything around us.

Comets are small balls of dusty ice that orbit the Sun. As they approach the Sun and are heated by it, gases evaporate from them and form a long tail.

Diameter is the width of a circle or sphere (ball). Planets are not perfect spheres – their diameter is measured across the equator.

Earthquakes are violent vibrations on the Earth's surface. These are caused by brittle rocks in the Earth's crust breaking up as plates in the crust rub and move against each other. This movement is sometimes called plate tectonics.

Energy enables things to do work. For example, the muscles in your body use energy every time you move around. There are many different forms of energy including heat, light, sound, electrical and chemical energy.

▲ Comet Kohoutek (in the centre) photographed on Christmas Day in 1973 from Skylab, high above Earth's atmosphere.

Equator is an imaginary line around a planet, midway between its north and south poles.

Gravity is a force that attracts objects to each other. It pulls us down towards Earth's surface. The more massive an object is, the greater its force of gravity.

Magnetic field is a region in which the effect of a magnet extends.

Milky Way is the star system, or galaxy, to which our solar system belongs.

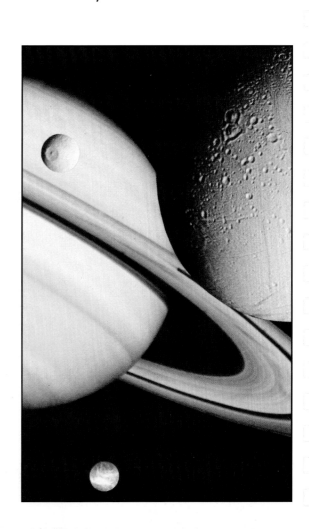

Index

APPLE MAC

1 Make sure that you have the minimum specification: (see Apple Macintosh specifications on page 40).

2 It is important that you do not have any other programs running. Before you start **INTERFACT**, click on the application menu in the top right-hand corner. Select each of the open applications and select Quit from the File menu.

COMMON PROBLEMS

Symptom: Cannot load disk.
Problem: There is not enough space available on your hard disk.
Solution: Make more space available by deleting old applications and programs you are not using.

Symptom: Disk will not run.
Problem: There is not enough memory available.
Solution: *Either* quit other applications and programs (see Quick Fixes) *or* increase your machine's RAM by adjusting the Virtual Memory.

Symptom: Graphics do not load or are poor quality.
Problem: *Either* there is not enough memory available *or* you have the wrong display setting.
Solution: *Either* quit other applications and programs (see Quick Fixes) *or* make sure that your monitor control is set to 256 colours (MAC) or VGA (PC).

Symptom: There is no sound (PCs only).
Problem: Your sound card is not Soundblaster compatible.
Solution: Configure sound settings to make them Soundblaster compatible (see your sound card manual for more information).

Symptom: Your machine freezes.
Problem: There is not enough memory available.
Solution: *Either* quit other applications and programs (see Quick Fixes) *or* increase your machine's RAM by adjusting the Virtual Memory.

Symptom: Text does not fit neatly into boxes and 'hot' words do not bring up extra information.
Problem: Standard fonts on your computer have been moved or deleted.
Solution: Re-install standard fonts. The PC version requires Arial; the Mac version requires Helvetica. See your computer manual for further information.

L

Troubleshooting

If you have a problem with your INTERFACT disk, you should find the solution here. You can also e-mail for help at helpline@two-canpublishing.com.

QUICK FIXES Run through these general checkpoints before consulting COMMON PROBLEMS (see opposite page).

QUICK FIXES

PC WITH WINDOWS 3.1 OR 3.11

1 Check that you have the minimum specification: (see PC specifications on page 40).

2 Make sure you have typed in the correct instructions: a colon (:) not a semi-colon (;) and a back slash (\) not a forward slash (/). Also, do not use punctuation or put any spaces between letters.

3 It is important that you do not have any other programs running. Before you start **INTERFACT**, hold down the Control key and press Escape. If you find that other programs are open, click on them with the mouse, then click the End Task key.

QUICK FIXES

PC WITH WINDOWS 95 or 98

1 Make sure you have typed in the correct instructions: a colon (:) not a semi-colon (;) and a back slash(\) not a forward slash (/). Also, do not use punctuation or put any spaces between letters.

2 It is important that you do not have any other programs running. Before you start **INTERFACT**, look at the task bar. If you find that other programs are open, click on them with the right mouse button and select Close from the pop-up menu.

DISK LINKS

When you read the book, you'll come across Disk Links. These show you where to find activities on the disk that relate to the page you are reading. Use the arrow keys to find the icon on screen that matches the one in the Disk Link.

DISK LINK
Save Alan the Astronaut by getting your space facts right when you play LOST IN SPACE!

BOOKMARKS

As you play the features on the disk, you'll bump into Bookmarks. These show you where to look in the book for more information about the topic on screen. Just turn to the page of the book shown in the Bookmark.

23

WORK BOOK

On pages 36–39 you'll find note pages to photocopy and use again and again. Use them to write down your own discoveries as you go through the book and the disk.

HOT DISK TIPS

- After you have chosen the feature you want to play, remember to move the cursor from the icon to the main screen before clicking on the mouse again.

- If you don't know how to use one of the on-screen controls, simply touch it with your cursor. An explanation will pop up in the reading box!

- Keep a close eye on the cursor. When it changes from an arrow ➔ to a hand ☞ click your mouse and something will happen.

- Any words that appear on screen in blue and are underlined are 'hot'. This means you can touch them with the cursor for more information.

- Explore the screen! There are secret hot spots and hidden surprises to find.

How to use INTERFACT

INTERFACT is easy to use.
First find out how to load the program
(see page 40) then read these simple
instructions and dive in!

You will find that there are lots of different features to explore. Use the controls on the right-hand side of the screen to selct the one you want to play. You will see that the main area of the screen changes as you click on to different features.

For example, this is what your screen will look like when you choose to play Rocket Mission, a journey of discovery through the solar system. Once you've selected a feature, click on the main screen to start playing.

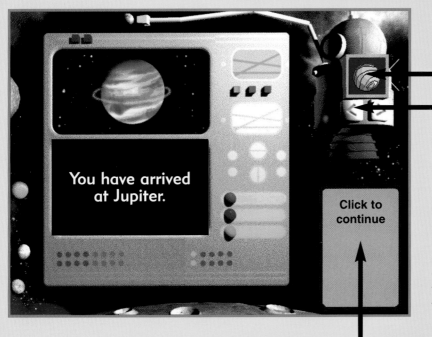

You have arrived at Jupiter.

Click to continue

Click here to select the feature you want to play.

Click on the arrow keys to scroll through the different features on the disk or find your way to the exit.

This is the reading box where instructions and directions appear explaining what to do. Go to page 4 to find out what's on the disk.

LOADING INSTRUCTIONS

You can run INTERFACT from the CD – you don't need to install it on your hard drive.

PC WITH WINDOWS 95 OR 98

The program should start automatically when you put the disk in the CD drive. If it does not, follow these instructions.

1. Put the disk in the CD drive
2. Open MY COMPUTER
3. Double-click on the CD drive icon
4. Double-click on the icon called SOLAR

PC WITH WINDOWS 3.1 OR 3.11

1. Put the disk in the CD drive
2. Select RUN from the FILE menu in the PROGRAM MANAGER
3. Type D:\ SOLAR (Where D is the letter of your CD drive)
4. Press the RETURN key

APPLE MACINTOSH

1. Put the disk in the CD drive
2. Double-click on the INTERFACT icon
3. Double-click on the icon called SOLAR

CHECKLIST

● Firstly, make sure that your computer and monitor meet the system requirements as set out on page 40.

● Ensure that your computer, monitor and CD-ROM drive are all switched on and working normally.

● It is important that you do not have any other applications, such as wordprocessors, running. Before starting INTERFACT quit all other applications.

● Make sure that any screen savers have been switched off.

● If you are running INTERFACT on a PC with Windows 3.1 or 3.11, make sure that you type in the correct instructions when loading the disk, using a colon (:) not a semi-colon (;) and a back slash (\) not a forward slash (/). Also, do not use any other punctuation or put any spaces between letters.

Loading your INTERFACT disk

INTERFACT is easy to load. But, before you begin, quickly run through the checklist on the opposite page to ensure that your computer is ready to run the program.

Your INTERFACT CD-ROM will run on both PCs with Windows and on Apple Macs. To make sure that your computer meets the system requirements, check the list below.

SYSTEM REQUIREMENTS

PC/WINDOWS
- Pentium 100Mhz processor
- Windows 95 or 98 (or later)
- 16Mb of RAM (24Mb recommended for Windows 98)
- VGA 256 colour monitor
- SoundBlaster-compatible soundcard
- 1Mb graphics card
- Double-speed CD-ROM drive

APPLE MACINTOSH
- 68020 processor (PowerMac or G3/iMac recommended)
- System 7.0 (or later)
- 16Mb of RAM
- Colour monitor set to at least 480 x 640 pixels and 256 colours
- Double-speed CD-ROM drive

Work book

Work book

▲ The planet Saturn with its rings and moons. This scene was compiled from Voyager 1 spacecraft photographs.

Moons are the natural objects that orbit a planet.

Radar is a system used to detect and locate objects that are hidden and cannot be seen.

Volcanoes are holes in a planet's crust where molten rock erupts.

SOLAR SYSTEM FACTS

● Our solar system condensed from a swirling cloud of dust and gas in one of the arms of a spiral galaxy called the **Milky Way** about 5 thousand million years ago.

● Neptune's largest **moon**, Triton, is falling towards Neptune. In ten million to 100 million years, Triton will collide with the planet.

● The planet with the strongest **gravity** is Jupiter. The force of gravity at its surface is 2.64 times Earth's. If it were possible to stand on Jupiter, someone weighing 50kg on Earth would weigh over 130kg on this massive planet.

● The closest star to the Sun is Proxima Centauri, a small, cool type of star called a 'red dwarf'. Travelling at the speed of light, it would take you 4.3 years to reach it.

● The closer a planet is to the Sun, the shorter its year. Mercury's year is 88 Earth-days long. Pluto's is 248 Earth-years long. Earth, which lies between the two, has 365.25 days in a year.

● The US Voyager 1 spacecraft discovered rings around Jupiter in 1979 and confirmed that the planets Uranus and Neptune are also encircled by rings.